Little Women

Louisa May Alcott

Level 1

Retold by M. Albers
Series Editors: Andy Hopkins and Jocelyn Potter

Pearson Education Limited
Edinburgh Gate, Harlow,
Essex CM20 2JE, England
and Associated Companies throughout the world.

Pack ISBN: 978-1-4058-5202-9
Book ISBN: 978-1-4058-4272-3
CD-ROM ISBN: 978-1-4058-5048-3

First published 1868
First published by Puffin Books 1953
This edition published 2007

5 7 9 10 8 6 4

Text copyright © Penguin Books Ltd 2000
This edition copyright © Pearson Education Ltd 2007
Illustrations by Gabriel León Bernstein

Set in 12.5/16pt A. Garamond
Printed in China
SWTC/04

Produced for the Publishers by AC Estudio Editorial S.L.

Published by Pearson Education Ltd in association with Penguin Books Ltd,
both companies being subsidiaries of Pearson Plc

For a complete list of the titles available in the Penguin Active Reading series please write to your local
Pearson Longman office or to: Penguin Readers Marketing Department. Pearson Education,
Edinburgh Gate, Harlow, Essex CM20 2JE, England.

Contents

1.1 What's the book about?

Read about this story on the back of this book. Then answer the questions.

1 How many girls are there in the March family?

....

2 Is their father at home with them?

....

3 Does the family have a lot of money?

....

4 Are the girls sometimes happy?

....

5 Is this a good year for them?

....

1.2 What happens first?

Look at the pictures on pages 1 and 2. What are the right answers? What do you think? Write them in the sentences.

1 The girls are ....

at work	at school	at home

2 The time of year is ....

Christmas	summer	fall

3 The girls are talking about ....

jobs	presents	boyfriends

4 They are thinking about their ...., too.

friends	brother	father

CHAPTER 1

A Letter from Father

"It's Christmas and we aren't going to have
any presents!" Jo said.

It was two days before Christmas.

Meg, Jo, Beth, and Amy March were sisters. Meg was sixteen and she was very beautiful. She had big eyes and beautiful long brown hair. Jo was fifteen. She was tall and thin. She had dark eyes and long brown hair. Beth was thirteen. She was very quiet. Little Amy had blue eyes and yellow hair.

It was six in the evening and the girls were at home. They talked about Christmas.

Jo wasn't happy.

"It's Christmas and we aren't going to have any **present**s!" she said.

Meg looked at her old dress.

"I know, Jo," she said. "But we don't have much money."

Amy said, "My friends are going to have presents. I want some presents, too."

Beth smiled.

"We don't have any money," she said. "But we have Mother and Father, and we're happy."

Jo didn't smile.

She said, "We don't have Father. He's away in the **war** and he isn't coming back for Christmas."

"Maybe he isn't going to come back," the girls **thought**. But they didn't say it.

---

present /'prezənt/ (n) Is that a *present* for me? Thank you!
war /wɔr/ (n) People in the two countries are angry. There is going to be a *war*.
thought /θɔt/ (v, past) I *thought* about my family but I did not visit them.

"We have a little money," Meg said. "What can we buy?"

"I want a new book," Jo said. She loved reading.

"And I'd like some pens," Amy said.

"I don't want any presents," Beth said. "Let's buy presents for Mother. We can put them on the table for her on Christmas Day."

"Yes," said Jo. "Let's do that. We can buy them tomorrow. What can we get for her?"

Then Mrs. March arrived in her dark coat and old hat.

She called, "Children, I'm home!"

"Hello, Mother!" the girls answered.

"Come and **kiss** me, girls!" Mrs. March said. They went to her, and she smiled at them. "I have a letter from Father," she said. "Let's eat, and then we can read it."

Later in the evening, Mrs. March said, "Sit down now, girls. I'm going to read Father's letter to you."

kiss /kɪs/ (v/n) *Kiss* your mother and then go to bed.

It was a happy letter. Father didn't talk about the war. The letter finished:

Give my love and a kiss to my little women. A year is a long time, but I think of them every day.

The girls were very unhappy. They wanted their father. They thought about his letter.

"I'm going to be good this year," Amy said.

"I don't like my work," Meg said, "but I'm going to do it well."

"I want to be a 'little woman' for Father," Jo said. "I'm often angry, but I'm going to stop now."

Beth didn't talk. She looked at the floor.

"Don't be unhappy, girls!" Mrs. March said. "Let's play a game."

After the game, Beth played the old **piano**. Then Mrs. March said, "Good night, girls. Sleep well!"

She kissed her daughters, and the four girls went up to bed.

piano /pi'ænoʊ/ (n) I can play the *piano*, but not well.

2.1 Were you right?

Look at your answers to Activity 1.2 on page iv. Then finish these
sentences with the words on the right.

1 The four sisters are   their mother.

2 They have no money   from their father.

3 They are waiting for   because they want their father.

4 They are talking about   Meg, Jo, Beth, and Amy.

5 Mrs. March brings a letter   his "little women."

6 Their father is writing   but they are a happy family.

7 The girls are unhappy   from the war.

8 Mr. March calls the girls   Christmas presents.

2.2 What more did you learn?

Write the girls' names under their pictures. Then write these words under
the right pictures.

plays the piano   beautiful   blue eyes   quiet   fifteen yellow hair   loves reading   tall and thin wants Christmas presents   thirteen   sixteen   big eyes

2.3 Language in use

Read the sentences in the box. Then finish these sentences with past tense verbs.

> She **was** very beautiful.
> They **talked** about Christmas.

1 Meg, Jo, Beth, and Amy .... sisters. (be)

2 Meg .... big eyes and beautiful brown hair. (have)

3 Jo .... fifteen. (be)

4 Mrs. March .... with a letter. (arrive)

5 She .... at her daughters. (smile)

6 The girls .... about their father. (think)

7 "Don't be unhappy, girls!" Mrs. March .... (say)

8 Beth .... the piano. (play)

2.4 What's next?

Look at the pictures on pages 6, 7, and 8. What do you think? Circle the right answer.

1 Amy gets *pens* / *a book* / *a dress* for Christmas.

2 Her present is under her *chair* / *table* / *bed*.

3 It is from *Jo* / *Mr. March* / *Mrs. March*.

4 There is a lot of *food* / *drink* / *candy* on the table.

5 The food is from *Santa Claus* / *Mrs. March* / *a family friend*.

6 The girls want to *give away* / *eat* / *try* the food.

5

CHAPTER 2

Christmas Day

Mrs. March said, "It's Christmas, girls. Can we give them our food?"

On Christmas morning, Meg, Jo, Beth, and Amy opened their eyes and looked under their beds. There were four books there. Meg's book was green, Jo's was red, Beth's was white, and Amy's was blue.

"Oh, Mother!" they thought. "You *are* good to us."

Meg opened her book and started to read it. Her sisters listened.

Later, they went down to the kitchen. Hannah was there. She lived in the house and she **help**ed Mrs. March. There was food on the table.

"Where's Mother?" Meg asked.

"I don't know," Hannah answered. "She went out very early."

Amy looked out the window.

"She's coming down the street!" she said.

"Quickly!" Jo said. "Put her presents away!"

Mrs. March came into the house.

"Good morning, Mother!" the girls called.

"Where were you?" Jo asked.

Mrs. March answered, "I went to Mrs. Hummel's house. She has seven small children. They don't have any food and they're very cold." She looked at her daughters. Then she said, "It's Christmas, girls. Can we give them our food?"

The girls looked at the food. They wanted to eat, but they said quickly, "Oh, yes, Mother. Can we take it?"

help /hɛlp/ (v) Please *help* me with my homework!

They went to the Hummels with a big bag of food.

Later in the morning, the girls said, "Here are your presents, Mother!"

"Oh! Thank you. You're good children," Mrs. March said. She looked at her presents and smiled.

◆

In the evening, the girls' friends came, and the girls **acted** for them. They loved acting and their friends had a good time.

Then Hannah said, "Come and eat, children!"

On the table there was a lot of food and some fruit and **candy**. The girls looked at it with open eyes. Where did it come from?

"It's from Santa Claus!" Beth said.

"No, Mother did it," Meg said.

Jo said, "It's from **Aunt** March! Maybe she likes us on Christmas Day. She doesn't usually like us."

act /ækt/ (v) He wants to *act* in movies.
candy /ˈkændi/ (n) The children want *candy*, but I only have fruit.
aunt /ænt, ɑnt/ (n) She visits her *aunt* every month.

7

"You're wrong," Mrs. March said. "It's from old Mr. Laurence. You see him sometimes—he lives near here."

"Yes, but we don't *know* him!" Meg said.

"He was a friend of my father," Mrs. March said. "He knows about the food for the Hummels. This food is for you from him because you didn't eat well this morning."

Jo's friend said, "My mother knows old Mr. Laurence. He's a good man, but he doesn't see many people. His daughter's dead and her son lives with him. The boy's name's Laurie."

"I want to meet Laurie," Jo said. "We don't know many boys. Maybe he can act."

"He can visit us," Mrs. March said.

Jo smiled.

"Oh," Beth said to her mother, "*we're* very happy. But Father isn't happy."

"No," Mrs. March said quietly. She kissed her daughter.

"I want to see him," Beth said. "I want to give him a present."

"I know, Beth. I know."

CHAPTER 3

The Party

"Oh!" said Jo. "A New Year's party!" "Yes," Meg said.
"But we don't have the right dresses."

F ive days later, Meg came quickly into the house.
"Jo! Jo!" she called. "Where are you?"

"Here," Jo called. "I'm reading."

Meg had a letter in her hand. "Listen. This letter's from Mrs.
Gardiner. It's for you and me, and it says, 'Please come to a small
party tomorrow evening.' I talked to Mother, and we can go."

"Oh!" said Jo. "A New Year's party!"

"Yes," Meg said. "But we don't have the right dresses."

Jo said, "And I have a **burn** on my good dress."

"You can sit on a chair all evening," Meg said. "Then people can't
see the burn. Don't dance!"

Before the party, Beth and Amy helped Meg and
Jo with their dresses and their hair.

"I can **curl** your hair with some hot curlers,
Meg," Jo said to her sister.

Suddenly, Beth said. "Oh, look—Meg's
hair! It's burning!"

"Oh! Oh! Oh!" Meg said. "My hair!
My hair! I can't go to the party now!"

But Amy said, "Put a **ribbon** in your
hair. There—you can't see the burn now."

Beth kissed Meg and said, "You're
beautiful."

party /ˈpɑrti/ (n) My brother is having a *party*. Please come.
burn /bɜːn/ (v) He *burned* the old table and chairs in the yard.
curl /kɜːl/ (v) My hair *curls*, but not in the rain. Do you have any *curlers*?
ribbon /ˈrɪbən/ (n) She always has red *ribbons* in her hair.

"Do you have your **glove**s, girls?" Mrs. March asked. "Good. Have a good time, and come home at eleven."

◆

At the party, the music played and Meg danced.

A tall boy with red hair walked across the room to Jo.

"Can we dance?" he asked her.

Jo wanted to dance, but she thought about the burn on her dress. She smiled and said "No."

Then she went quickly into a small, quiet room. But the Laurence boy was there.

"Oh! I *am* sorry," Jo said. "I didn't see you." She looked at him. "You live in the big house near our house. My name's Josephine March, but people call me Jo."

The boy smiled. "Hello. I'm Laurie," he said.

"Laurie Laurence?" Jo asked.

"My name's Theodore," he said. "But I don't like it because boys called me 'Dora.' Now I'm Laurie."

"We loved your Christmas present," Jo said. "Do you like parties?"

glove /glʌv/ (n) Take your *gloves*. It is very cold today.

"Sometimes. I was in France for years, and I don't know people here."

"France!" Jo said. "Can you talk French?"

Jo and Laurie talked and talked. Laurie liked music.

"Listen to the piano!" Jo said. "Let's go and dance."

"Yes, let's do that," Laurie said.

"Oh!" Jo said suddenly. "I can't—"

"Why?" Laurie asked.

"I have a burn in the back of my dress. I can't dance."

Laurie smiled. "People aren't going to look," he said. "Please come."

◆

The party finished and Jo and Meg went home. They went up to their bedroom. Amy and Beth were in bed, but they quickly opened their eyes.

Amy said, "Did you have a good time?"

"Oh, yes," Meg said.

"And you, Jo?" Beth asked.

"Yes, I had a good time, too," Jo said. "Here's some candy from the party."

They talked for a long time about the party and about Laurie.

3.1 Were you right?

Look at your answers to Activity 2.4. Then read these sentences. Are they right (✓) or wrong (✗)?

1 Meg's book is red and Jo's is green. ◯

2 The girls do not like their presents. ◯

3 The girls take food to the Hummel family. ◯

4 Mrs. Hummel has six children. ◯

5 The girls give their mother presents. ◯

6 The girls love acting with their friends. ◯

7 Aunt March sends fruit and candy. ◯

8 Mr. Laurence's daughter lives with him. ◯

3.2 What more did you learn?

Look at the pictures and answer the questions. Write the people's names.

1 Who gets a letter about a party? ....

2 Who burns her sister's hair? ....

3 Who looks beautiful? ....

4 Who is tall with red hair? ....

5 Who has a burn on her dress? ....

6 Who knows French? ....

7 Who dances with Laurie? ....

3.3 Language in use

Read the sentence in the box. Then write these words in the sentences.

There was a lot of food **on** the table.

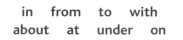

| in | from | to | with |
| about | at | under | on |

1 The book is .... Amy's bed.

2 The letter is .... Mrs. Gardiner.

3 Jo has a burn .... her dress.

4 Meg and Jo go .... the party.

5 Laurie lived .... France for years.

6 Jo dances .... Laurie.

7 Beth and Amy stay .... home.

8 Meg and Jo talk .... Laurie.

3.4 What's next?

Look at the pictures on pages 14, 15, and 16. Read the words under the name of the chapter. What do you think?

1 Who lives in the big house?

....

2 Who does Jo see at the window?

....

3 What is Laurie saying to Jo?

....

4 What is Jo looking at in the room?

....

5 Who gets a present of a piano?

....

CHAPTER 4

The Laurences

"I had a little girl with your eyes," he said to her one day.
"She played the piano, too. She was Laurie's mother."

O ne cold morning, Meg and Jo didn't want to get up.
"I don't want to work today," Meg said.

"I want to stay at home, too," Jo said, "but we can't do that."

Meg was the teacher for four children in the King family. The job was difficult, because the children only wanted to play.

Jo worked at Aunt March's house. Aunt March was Father's sister, but she had a lot of money. Jo liked her house because she had a lot of books. But Aunt March was an angry woman, and Jo didn't always like her.

Amy went to school every day. Beth was a very quiet girl and she didn't want to go to school. She helped Hannah in the house and she had a teacher at home.

In the afternoon, Jo came home from Aunt March's house. She looked up at the Laurences' big house. Laurie was at a window.

Jo called, "Hello. How are you? Are you sick?"

Laurie answered, "No, I *was* sick, but now I'm well again. Come and talk to me."

Jo went into Laurie's house and they talked.

Jo thought, "Laurie doesn't see many people—only old Mr. Laurence and his teacher, Mr. Brooke."

"What are you thinking, Miss Jo?" Laurie said.

She answered, "Come and visit us. You can meet Mother and my sisters. Beth can play the piano and Amy can dance for you. Meg and I can talk to you."

Laurie smiled. "I'd like that," he said.

There was a noise at the door. Then Laurie said, "Excuse me, the doctor's here. Can you wait?"

"Yes, of course," Jo said.

In the room there was a picture of Mr. Laurence. Jo looked at it and said, "His face isn't very friendly, but I like him."

"Thank you," said a man behind her.

It was old Mr. Laurence! Jo's face was very red, but the old man smiled.

"How do you do?" he said. "Come and sit with me."

Laurie came back, and Jo talked about her family with him and Mr. Laurence.

After this visit, the March girls often played at Laurie's house and he came to their home. Beth often played the piano there. It was a good piano, and Mr. Laurence liked listening to her music.

"I had a little girl with your eyes," he said to her one day. "She played the piano, too. She was Laurie's mother."

Then one day there was a piano in the March family's front yard. The letter on it said, "To Miss Elizabeth March."

"For me!" Beth said.

"Yes, it's a present for you from Mr. Laurence," Jo said.

Quiet little Beth went quickly to the big house.

"Thank you! Thank you!" she said to the old man.

Then she kissed him.

After that, the Marches and the Laurences were very good friends.

CHAPTER 5

Problems for Amy

Amy closed her eyes, and Mr. Davis hit her hand.
"Now stand here at my table," he said. "Don't move."

"I want some money," Amy said one day. "It's important."

"Why, Amy?" Meg asked.

"Every day my friends take candy to school. I eat their candy, but I can't buy it for *them*."

"Here's a little money for you," Meg said. "But please don't ask again. We don't have a lot of money, you know."

"Oh, thank you, Meg," Amy said.

In the morning, at school, Amy had the candy in her bag. Now every girl wanted to be Amy's friend.

Katy Brown said, "Please come to my party."

Then Jenny Snow said, "Can I have some candy? I can help you with your schoolwork."

"No, you can't have any candy," Amy said. "Yesterday you said, 'Amy March is fat!'"

She walked away.

Jenny Snow was angry, and she went to the teacher.

"Mr. Davis," she said. "Amy March has some candy in her school bag."

Mr. Davis was angry, too. He didn't like candy at school.

"Amy March," he said. "Come here. Bring me your candy."

Amy walked to Mr. Davis's table at the front of the room.

He said, "Never bring candy to school again! Do you hear me?"

"Yes, Mr. Davis," Amy said.

Then he said, "Your hand, Miss March."

Amy closed her eyes, and Mr. Davis **hit** her hand.

"Now stand here at my table," he said. "Don't move."

Amy's face was red and she was very unhappy.

Later, the teacher said, "You can sit down now, Miss March."

But Amy didn't sit down. She didn't talk to Mr. Davis or the girls. She was angry and unhappy. She went home.

hit /hɪt/ (v, past) The car *hit* a tree and stopped.

"Amy, what's wrong?" Mrs. March asked. "Why are you home from school early?"

Amy said, "Mr. Davis hit me because I had candy at school."

Mrs. March was angry now.

"Mr. Davis hit you!" she said. "That's not right, and I'm going to write a letter to the school. You can stay at home. Beth's teacher can teach you, too."

"Good!" Amy said.

"But Amy," Mrs. March said, "you were bad. Mr. Davis doesn't like candy at school, and you know that."

Amy thought about that. Then she said, "Yes, I wasn't very good. I wanted to be important, and that was wrong. I'm sorry."

Amy's mother and her sisters looked at her and smiled.

4.1 Were you right?

Look at your answers to Activity 3.4. Then look at these people. What are they thinking? Put these words in the sentences.

| present | friendly | talk | eyes | piano | like | daughter | face |

My .... played the piano. Beth has her ....

1

I .... Jo. I want to .... to her.

2

Is this beautiful .... a .... for me?

3

His .... isn't .... , but I like him.

4

4.2 What more did you learn?

What comes first in Chapter 5? Number the sentences, 1–8.

a Amy goes home. ◯

b Every girl wants to be Amy's friend. ◯

c Jenny Snow is angry with Amy. ◯

d Amy is sorry. ◯

e Meg gives Amy money for candy. ①

f Mrs. March is angry with Mr. Davis. ◯

g Mr. Davis hits Amy's hand. ◯

h Amy takes candy to school. ◯

4.3 Language in use

Read the sentences in the box. Then write *can* or *can't* in these sentences.

> Amy **can** dance for you.
>
> You **can't** have any candy.

1 Beth .... play the piano very well.

2 Amy has no money. She .... buy candy.

3 "............... I have some candy?" Jenny Snow asked. "I .... help you with your homework."

4 "No, you .... ," Amy said.

5 "You .... stay at home with Beth," Mrs. March said.

4.4 What's next?

Look at the words in *italics* on page 22 and at this picture. What do you think? Put the right words in these sentences.

1 The time of year is ....

| summer | fall | winter |

2 Amy is in the ....

| ocean | river | boat |

3 The ice is very ....

| strong | heavy | thin |

4 The water is very ....

| hot | cold | light |

5 Amy is .... to Jo and Laurie.

| calling | running | swimming |

CHAPTER 6

Amy is Angry Again

The ice was thin there and suddenly—CRACK!
She went down into the cold water.

"Meg, Jo, where are you going?" Amy asked one Saturday afternoon.

"You can't come, Amy!" Jo said.

"I know!" Amy said. "You're going to the theater with Laurie. I'm coming, too! I have a little money."

"It isn't for little girls," Jo said. "And Laurie asked *us*."

Amy was very angry.

"You're going to be sorry, Jo March," she said.

Then Laurie arrived, and Meg and Jo went to the theater with him.

◆

In the morning, Jo asked, "Where's my book?"

Jo liked writing stories, and she was a good writer. There was many years' work in that book.

Meg and Beth said, "We don't know."

Amy was quiet.

"Do you have it, Amy?" Jo asked.

"No, I don't," Amy said.

"Amy ...!" Jo said. "Where is it?"

"I burned it!" Amy answered.

"You burned my book!" said Jo, "My stories were in it! You bad girl!"

She hit Amy and walked away.

Later, Jo came down again.

"I'm very, very sorry, Jo!" Amy said.

But Jo didn't look at her.

In the evening, Mrs. March talked to Jo.

"Amy did a very bad thing," she said. She kissed her daughter. "But please be friends with her. Don't be angry now."

"I don't like her, and I don't want to be friends," Jo answered, and she went to bed.

◆

The morning after that, Jo thought, "I want to be happy today. I'm going to go **ice skating** with Laurie."

She and Laurie walked down the road with their skates. Amy watched them. She wanted to go, too.

Meg said to her, "Go after them. Kiss Jo, and say 'sorry' again."

Amy walked to the river behind Jo and Laurie. Then Jo and Laurie started to skate, and Amy skated, too. Jo didn't look at her and Laurie didn't see her.

Then Amy moved away from them. The ice was thin there and suddenly—CRACK! She went down into the cold water.

"Help! Help me!" Amy called.

Jo looked now.

ice /aɪs/ (n) Drive slowly! There is *ice* on the roads.
skate /skeɪt/ (v/n) In winter people *skate* on the rivers. Do you have any *skates*?

"Oh, no! Amy!" she said. "We're coming, Amy!"

Jo and Laurie quickly helped Amy out of the water. She was very cold. Her face and hands were blue.

They went home quickly, and Hannah went to Amy's bedroom with her.

Later, Jo was in Amy's room with her mother. They talked quietly.

"Is Amy going to get well?" Jo asked.

"Yes," Mrs. March said. "You came home very quickly. You helped her."

Jo said, "I was very angry with Amy, but now I'm sorry. I'm often angry. What can I do?"

She looked at her sister. She was beautiful with her yellow hair. Amy opened her eyes and looked at Jo. They kissed, and they were friends again.

"Jo," said Mother, "you *are* very angry sometimes. You can stop that. Please try! But you're a good girl, and I love you."

Jo kissed her mother.

Meg's Glove

*Mrs. March looked quickly at her daughter. Meg was
very beautiful, but she was a child.*

I n the summer, Laurie said to the March girls, "Let's put a letter **box**
in the tree in front of your house. Then I can send you letters."

The girls liked the box. Beth opened it every day.

One day she said, "There's a letter for Miss Amy."

"Thank you," Amy said.

"There are two letters for Miss Jo—and a very old hat!"

"I burn my face every day in this sun," Jo said. "Laurie's
a good boy."

"And there's a present for Miss Meg March."

"It's a letter—and my glove," Meg said. "But there's only *one*
glove. I had two gloves at the Laurences' house yesterday."

box /bɑks/ (n) My letters are in a *box* under my bed.

"There was only one glove in the box," Beth said. "Were you with Mr. Brooke yesterday?"

"Yes," Meg said. "He wanted to read a story to me."

Mrs. March looked quickly at her daughter. Meg was very beautiful, but she was a child. Her mother smiled.

◆

That summer was a happy time, but winter came. In October the days were cold and short.

Jo was in the house one day. She looked at the little book in front of her.

"There!" she said. "I can take it now."

She went quietly out of the window. Her mother and sisters didn't see her.

Jo went to an office in town. Laurie was in town, too, and he waited for her. She came out into the street, and her face was red.

"What's wrong?" Laurie asked.

"I went to the newspaper office with two stories," Jo said. "The man said, 'Come again in a week.' He's going to read them."

"That's very good!" Laurie said. "Josephine March, the famous American writer! But Jo, I want to talk to you about Meg's glove—I know about it."

"Where *is* the glove?" Jo asked.

"It's in Mr. Brooke's coat," Laurie said.

"Oh no!" Jo thought. "Mr. Brooke loves Meg! He's going to take her away from us!"

◆

Two weeks later, Jo came into the house with a newspaper.

"Are there any good stories in the newspaper?" Meg asked.

"Yes," Jo answered. "There's one good story."

"Please read it to us," Amy said.

The three sisters listened.

"It's good! Who's the writer?" Beth asked.

"Your sister." Jo smiled.

"You!" Meg said.

"Yes, me!"

"It's *very* good!" Amy said.

"Oh, Jo!" Hannah said.

Mother smiled and kissed her daughter. "Father's going to be very happy."

5.1 Were you right?

Look at your answers to Activity 4.4. Then finish the sentences with the words on the right.

1 Jo is angry ·················· because she wants to say sorry.
2 Jo goes skating because it is very thin.
3 Jo doesn't look at Amy because Jo and Amy are friends again.
4 Amy walks behind Jo because she is angry with her.
5 The ice goes CRACK ················ because Amy burned her book.
6 Mrs. March is happy because she wants to be happy.

5.2 What more did you learn?

Look at these pictures. How are these things important in the story? Write the words.

 A

 B

 C

 D

 E

1 Mr. Brooke has this in his coat. ....
2 Laurie sends this to Jo. ....
3 The girls and Laurie put letters in this. ....
4 Jo writes stories in this. ....
5 Amy has these for skating. ....

5.3 Language in use

Read the sentence in the box. Then make sentences with _going to_.

> Is Amy **going to get** well?

1 Jo's face ...._is going to burn_........ in the sun. (burn)

2 Amy and Beth .... at home. (stay)

3 The man in the newspaper office .... Jo's stories. (read)

4 I .... ice skating. (go)

5 "You .... sorry, Jo!" said Amy. (be)

6 .... Mr. March .... happy? (be)

5.4 What's next?

1 **What is the name of Chapter 8?**

    ....

2 **Look at the pictures on pages 30 and 31. Circle the right words. What do you think?**

   a Mrs. March is reading a _newspaper_ / _book_ / _letter._

   b She is looking _happy_ / _unhappy_ / _angry._

   c The letter is about _Mr. March_ / _Mr. Laurence_ / _Aunt March._

   d Jo's hair is very _long_ / _short_ / _yellow._

   e Jo is looking _happy_ / _unhappy_ / _angry._

CHAPTER 8

Jo's Hair

"Jo—your hair!" Mrs. March said. Jo's hair was very short. "What did you do?"

The letter arrived in early November. Laurie was at the March house with the girls and their mother.
The letter said:

Mrs. March,
Mr. March is in Washington and he is very sick. Please come quickly.
From, S. Hale.

The girls were very unhappy. Mrs. March's face was white.
"Children, listen to me!" she said. "Help me, please. Laurie, please write to Mr. Hale. I'm going to take the morning train."
"Yes, Mrs. March," Laurie said.
"Jo, take a letter to Aunt March. I'm going to ask her for money. Beth, ask Mr. Laurence for food and drink for Mr. March. Amy, get my black bag. Meg, come and help me."
Later, Mr. Brooke came to the house.

He said to Meg, "Miss March, I want to go with your mother tomorrow. I can do some work for Mr. Laurence in Washington, too."

"Thank you," Meg said. "Mother would like that."

Mrs. March came in.

"Yes, thank you, Mr. Brooke," she said. Then she asked, "Where's Jo?"

The front door opened. It was Jo.

"Jo—your hair!" Mrs. March said. Jo's hair was very short. "What did you do?"

"Aunt March is reading your letter," she said. "But here's some money for Father from me. I went to a man in town. He buys hair."

"Oh, Jo, thank you," Mrs. March said. "I love you for this."

Jo smiled at her mother, but that night she didn't sleep.

"What's wrong, Jo?" Meg asked.

"My hair!" Jo said. Her eyes were red. "My hair!"

CHAPTER 9

Beth is Sick

*"The child was dead. It was scarlet fever. And
now I'm sick, too."*

T he girls said goodbye to their mother. Every day they did their
work, but they thought about her.

One day, Beth said to Jo and Meg, "Please go and see the Hummels."

"I can't go. Can you go, Jo?" Meg asked.

"No, I have a cold," Jo answered.

"Can you go, Beth?" Meg asked.

"I go every day, because Mother isn't here. But one child is very
sick and I can't help her. Please go."

"I can go tomorrow," Meg said.

Beth went to the Hummel's house. Later, she came home. She was
very unhappy.

"What's wrong, Beth?" Jo asked.

"Oh, Jo. The child's dead. I stayed with her and Mrs. Hummel
went to the doctor's house. He came, but
the child was dead. It was **scarlet fever**.
And now I'm sick, too."

"Oh, no!" Jo said. "I'm going
to get Hannah."

Hannah looked at Beth and
called Dr. Bangs.

"Amy," Jo said, "you're going
to Aunt March's house."

"No!" Amy said.

"Yes," Hannah said. "Do you
want scarlet fever?"

scarlet fever /ˌskɑrlɪt ˈfivər/ (n) The children had *scarlet fever* and now one of them is dead.

Later in the week, Beth was very sick. Jo stayed with her. She washed her sister's face and talked to her. But Beth didn't know Jo, Meg, or Hannah. Jo wanted her mother, but her father was sick, too. They didn't write to Mrs. March about Beth.

Dr. Bangs came every day. One day, he looked at Beth and said, "Please write to Mrs. March now."

Then Laurie came to the house.

"Your mother knows about Beth," he said. "Your father isn't very sick now, and she's coming home this evening. I didn't wait—"

"Oh, Laurie!" Jo said. "Thank you!"

In Beth's bedroom, Meg and Jo looked at Beth's face. It was white.

Jo thought, "Oh, no, my sister's dead!" She kissed her and said, "Goodbye, Beth, goodbye."

But Hannah looked at the child and smiled.

"Beth isn't dead," she said. "She's sleeping! She's going to be well again!"

There was a noise at the door.

"Listen, girls!" Hannah said.

Laurie called, "She's here! Mrs. March is home!"

6.1 Were you right?

Look at your answers to Activity 5.4. Are your answers right? Who says these words? Who are they talking to? Write the letters, A–E.

 A

 B

 C

 D

 E

1 "Please write to Mr. Hale." ◯ ◯

2 "Take a letter to Aunt March." ◯ ◯

3 "I want to go with your mother." ◯ ◯

4 "Here's some money for Father from me." ◯ ◯

5 "I love you for this." ◯ ◯

6.2 What more did you learn?

Are these sentences right (✓) or wrong (✗)?

1 Meg goes to the Hummels' house. ◯

2 The Hummel boy is dead from scarlet fever. ◯

3 Beth gets sick from scarlet fever. ◯

4 Jo sends Amy to Mr. Laurence's house. ◯

5 Jo writes to Mrs. March. ◯

6 Mrs. March comes home. ◯

6.3 Language in use

Read the sentence in the box. Write negative sentences.

> They **didn't write** to Mrs. March about Beth.

1 Meg went to the Hummels' house.
  Meg didn't go to the Hummels' house

2 Beth talked to her sisters.

3 Amy wanted to go to Aunt March's house.

4 Mr. Laurence came to the house.

5 Beth was dead.

6 Mr. March came home.

6.4 What's next?

1 In Chapter 10 the March family get a big Christmas present. What is the present? What do you think?

2 Look at the pictures in Chapter 10. Who is thinking these words? What do you think? Write the names.

a "I'm sick—but very happy."

b "I don't want Aunt March's money."

c "I'm never going to come back to this house!"

d "I love Meg and I want to marry her."

What is Love?

"And here's a big Christmas present for the March family!" Laurie said.

Mrs. March came into the room. Meg and Jo kissed her. Then Beth slowly opened her eyes and smiled.

Mrs. March stayed with her all night. In the morning, Jo went into Beth's room.

"Mother, I want to talk to you," she said. "Mr. Brooke loves Meg. Did you know that? I don't like it."

"I know," Mrs. March said. "John Brooke talked to your father and me in Washington. Does Meg love him, too?"

"I don't know," Jo said. "I don't know about love. I liked Mr. Brooke's letters about Father, and I like his eyes. But I want Meg here, at home with us."

"John's a very good man," said Mrs. March. "He helped Father. But don't think about it now. Christmas is coming."

◆

On Christmas Day, Beth was in bed but Amy was home again. It was a good day. There were beautiful presents from Laurie and Mr. Laurence.

Then Laurie arrived.

"And here's a *big* Christmas present for the March family!" he said.

He opened the door again, and there was Mr. March. The girls went to their father and kissed him. They were very, very happy.

"Quietly, girls!" Mrs. March said. "Beth is sleeping!"

But Beth came down from her bedroom.

"Oh, Father, it's you!" she said.

◆

In the morning, Mr. Brooke talked to Meg.

"I love you," he said. "Do you love me?"

"I'm only seventeen," Meg said. "I don't know ..."

Then Aunt March came into the room. Mr. Brooke went out quickly.

"Where are your mother and father?" Aunt March said. "And what's that man saying to you?"

"He's father's friend, Aunt March!" Meg said.

"Then why is your face red?" Aunt March said. "You can't **marry** *him*. He doesn't have any money! I'm not going to give you *my* money."

Meg was very angry.

"I don't want your money, Aunt March! John loves me, and he's a good man. We can work for our money. I *am* going to marry him."

---

marry /'mæri/ (v) I love him and I am going to *marry* him.

"Marry him, then! I don't want to see you again!"

Aunt March walked out of the house.

Meg didn't move. She looked out the window at her aunt's back.

Mr. Brooke came into the room again.

"My love—I listened. Thank you, thank you," he said. "Can I ask you again ...?"

Meg looked into his eyes.

"Oh, John, the answer's *yes*. I'm going to marry you—and we're going to be very happy."

◆

Later, Jo talked to Laurie.

"I love Meg, and I want her with me," she said. "But she's going to be happy, and that's good. And *I'm* happy today. Mother and Father are here. Beth is well again. Meg loves John. Amy and I are friends—and you and I are friends, too. I'm writing, and people like my stories. But Laurie, are we going to be happy in a year, or in two years? Who knows?"

1 **Work with three friends. Look at the pictures. These people are thinking about Meg and John.**

a What are they thinking? What do you think?

b Put these words in the right places in the sentences.

> too   important   money   friend   home   happy

Aunt March: "I don't like John Brooke. He has no ...."

Mrs. March: "Money is not .... John can make a good .... for Meg."

Jo: "I am not .... about John Brooke. I want Meg to stay with us."

Laurie: "Jo loves Meg. But John loves Meg, ... I can always be Jo's ...."

c You are Aunt March, Mrs. March, Jo, and Laurie. Talk about Meg and John Brooke. What do you think?

2 **Talk about these people. Who are they? Are they good people? Why are they important in the story?**

a Mr. Laurence
b the Hummel family
c Mr. Davis
d Laurie

e John Brooke
f Mr. March
g Dr. Bangs

You are Mr. Laurence. Write a letter to Mrs. March about Beth. Put these words in the right places.

| daughters | every | house | stayed | scarlet fever | dead |
| | family | problems | sick | quickly | |

November 25

Mrs. March,

I am very sorry, but there are .... at home.

Beth visited the Hummel .... and one child

was very sick. She had ....

Beth .... with her and Mrs. Hummel went to

the doctor's house. He came, but the child was

....

Now Beth is very ...., too. Meg and Jo are

with her, but she doesn't know them. Amy is

at Aunt March's .... Dr. Bangs

comes .... day. Your .... want you

very much. Please come home ....

Yours,

41

1 Work with two or three friends. The man at the newspaper wants to write about Jo in his newspaper. What questions does he ask? Write the words in the right places.

sisters	boyfriend	old	many	live	job	like	name

a What's your .... ?

b How .... are you?

c How .... brothers and .... do you have?

d Where do you .... ?

e What do you .... doing?

f Do you have a .... ?

g What .... do you want to do?

2 Write Jo's answers to the questions. Put words on the left with words on the right.

Jo March.

I am

I don't have

in a town in America.

I like

a boyfriend.

I have

three sisters.

My name is

fifteen.

I live

I want to be

writing stories and skating.

a famous writer

a My name is Jo March. ....

b ....

c ....

d ....

e ....

f ....

g ....

3 **Talk to three friends. Ask these questions and write the answers.**

Student A

What's your name? ....

How old are you? ....

How many brothers and sisters do you have? ....

Where do you live? ....

What do you like doing? ....

Do you have a girlfriend/boyfriend? ....

What job do you do/want to do? ....

Student B

What's your name? ....

How old are you? ....

How many brothers and sisters do you have? ....

Where do you live? ....

What do you like doing? ....

Do you have a girlfriend/boyfriend? ....

What job do you do/want to do? ....

Student C

What's your name? ....

How old are you? ....

How many brothers and sisters do you have? ....

Where do you live? ....

What do you like doing? ....

Do you have a girlfriend/boyfriend? ....

What job do you do/want to do? ....

4 **Read about Jo in the newspaper.**

Jo March: A New Writer

This is Jo March. She is fifteen. She has three sisters. She lives in our town in America. She likes writing stories and skating. She doesn't have a boyfriend. She wants to be a famous writer.

Write about your three friends.

....: ....

This is ....

....

....

....

....: ....

This is ....

....

....

....

....: ....

This is ....

....

....

....